Summat n'

An Airedale Anthology

By Gordon Dean

Studio Cottage Publications

Dedicated to Norman Cree, and all past, present and future members of Hall Royd Band

ISBN 0-9541638-0-X

First published in 2001 by Studio Cottage Publications

T' Band Marathon

I've been asked by our conductor
  to write a poem or two,
and thought of t'Lion and Albert
  and t'adventures at the zoo

But why, I thought, should Blackpool
  get all the fame and glory?
Charity begins at home,
  so here's another story

There's a little place called Shipley
  not far from Bradford Town
that hosts a Band o' Brasses
  playing notes reet up and down

This band is for young people
  from seven to seventy five
and by gum, when they
blow their horns
  it's good to be alive

They have a grand conductor
  his name is Norman Cree
and when he starts conducting,
  by, what a sight to see!

His arms go here,
  his arms go theer,
and t'band tries hard to cope.
  As music goes on faster
they've little left but hope

Sometimes its 80 beats to t'minute
  - at times near double that,
and when you're playing that speed,
  you've little time to chat!

The horns are playing crotchets,
  the trombones playing quavers,
and Alex' playing owt he can
  to gain t'conductor's favours

Remorselessly the piece goes on
  and many throats are dry.
'Only seventy more bars left'
  says Rosalind with a sigh

At last its nearly ovver -
  half t'band are on the floor,
and even them still sitting
  are shaken to the core

Just another fourteen bars
  and then we'll have a rest.
But Norman's arms move quicker
  and quite obscure his chest!

Its touch and go, its touch and go,
  whether they'll last out;
a funny sound, they all look round
  and Peter's just passed out!

But with a mighty struggle
  and blowing fit to bust,
they finish t'piece when Norman does
  but by gum - only just!

Festival Day

T'wert' Cleckley Textile Festival
and t'day of Big Parade.
Branston Band were there i'strength,
and all their plans were made

The starting point were Elmly Park.
The route on Bradfield Lane.
Then two miles t'Cathedral,
so they hoped it wouldn't rain

Now t'Committee had informed 'em
that they'd be to the fore.
so they'd practised marching
up and down,
until their feet were sore

Imagine their surprise, then,
when turning up on t'day,
to find parked out in front of 'em
a well known brewer's dray

Beautifully painted,
it really was a treat,
and pulled by two gert horses
with fluff all round their feet

It seemed that t'mayor and lady wife
would travel on the dray
so they could wave to t'populace,
who'd cheer and shout 'hurray'

Well, time came round to start t'parade,
and t'dray set off quite smart,
wi t' Branston Band and t'other groups
invited to take part

Peter at left marker
hugged 'B' flat Bass to t'chest,
and set off very crisply,
an example to the rest

Nar there's thousands live i' Cleckley,
and most of 'em were there -
but not on Bradfield Lane,
which looked a trifle bare

And it weren't that long
before the Band
found a snag they hadn't thowt of,
as t'horses dropped their little piles
in nice neat lines - well sort of!

So big Jim did a sidestep
to miss the fresh manure,
and little Tim a funny dance
to get in step once more

Now t'music's nearly up your nose,
and bouncing up and down,
so it's very hard to play and march
particularly in town

Gordon, no Harry Mortimer
by his own admission,
just couldn't focus on the notes
(he needs a good optician)

But on they went quite brightly
with Rosalind out of puff,
and notes a little hit and miss
but by and large, good stuff

As 'top of Bankside came and went,
it seemed they'd walked for miles,
and as they progressed bravely,
t'horses made more piles

So big Jim sidestepped yet again
to miss the fresh manure,
and little Tim did t'funny dance
to get in step once more

Band finally reached 'Cathedral
and as they stood at ease,
they heard crisp martial music
come wafting on the breeze

Some said 'Brighouse and Rastrick'
Others 'Black Dyke or such'
but after all their efforts
it didn't please them much

Hours of endeavour,
and t'music carefully planned,
and then to be upstaged
by a really famous Band

But when it finally came in sight
to cries of 'flipping heck'
all it was was a small blue truck
and a mobile discotheque!

Another great occasion then,
and all were glad they'd been
- and in spite of t'horses efforts
Jim's shoes were ***still*** quite clean!

Paintin' t'Band Trailer

It were Norman's idea and it seemed
quite a good'n;
  a party to paint the band trailer.
An' although when t'call came
  it were really quite sudden,
at least t'job wasn't a failure

Just twenty-four hours were
all that we got
  to turn up wi' scrapers and brushes.
(Misen, I thought we'd lose
Alex and Mark,
  who'd be kicking a ball round
  the bushes)

But no, as we got to
H.Q. at Drub Lane,
  the trailer were almost submerged,
with all t'nine of us sanding the front,
sides and back,
  mekking sure the old blue paint
  was purged

To say it were busy were gross
understatement,
  it were really a scene o' congestion
and wi' nine busy folks all doing
their thing
  good team work were
  art a' the question

On t'offside were three of us painting
quite slowly,
  an' having a really good session.
On t'nearside however, paint's
splashing all ovver,
  as t'other six tried self-expression

But as time went on,
so did the white paint,
  though not allus on to the van.
And by t'look of some of our clothing
and faces
  you'd ha' thowt we'd been
  swimming in t'can

Norman was leeting
the barbecue now
  and he didn't rub
  two sticks together,
but put all 'twigs in a
wigwam-like pile -
  he thowt they would go
  'ell for leather!

But ten minutes later,
and no sign of a glow
  we decided we needed to cheat,
so we placed a firelighter in t'middle
at' fuel,
  standing back to avoid intense heat!

But t'firelighter just sat as we
watched it i' vain,
and steadfastly refused to combust -
and as it were purchased
in very good faith
we thought this a trifle unjust!

So Norman decided to takk
a short stroll
his object to get lot's more wood.
(Situation was getting
quite desperate now,
as t'painters were baying for food)

At last wi' twelve newspapers plus
lots o' small twigs,
the charcoal began to ignite.
With our stomachs thinking our
throats had been cut,
this of course was a marvellous sight

Losing no time now all systems
were go,
Christine quickly put
nine burgers out,
though the twigs were still only
smouldering,
wi' woodsmoke still billowing out

It was now that Andrew took ovver
as chef
and straight away showed
much panache
by dropping all t'burgers through t'grill
onto t'fire,
where they got rather covered with ash!

Na' when Dawdler turned up for his
food i' white gloves,
good manners, it seemed were
still in.
But the answer was really far simpler
he'd paint ovver most of his skin

The bangers and burgers were very
soon gone,
some a trifle affected by smoke,
but mixed with the smell and the taste
of white gloss
we all took it as rather a joke

The painting complete and the
mudguards replaced,
gleaming white from the front
to the rear,
we decided 'UN' on the side would
look good -
or even 'Fresh Ice Creams served here'

So the final part of the ordeal began -
it was now time to clean the mess up.
Nine brushes completely covered
i' paint;
and white spirit?
Well we'd nobbut a cup!

But at last all was done and we set off
for home.
Still everywhere paint seemed to lurk;
in fact there were quite a lot less
on the trailer
than on them who'd done all the work!

You can't beat a good Brass Band

Now I love all kinds of music,
  from symphony to jazz.
I like the great welsh choirs
  and the rock and roll pzazz.
I even like the bagpipes,
  in fact I think they're grand,
but you can't beat the sound
  of a good Brass Band

Once or twice I've been abroad,
  to places near and far,
and enjoyed the German Umpah bands
  whilst supping up a 'jar'.
I love the Swiss and yodelling
  but you must understand
that you can't beat the sound
  of a good Brass Band

There's Caribbean Reggae
  and of course the Motown Sound.
There's Haydn, Bach and Mozart,
  there's lots of music round.
But if you want it at its best,
  whether live or canned,
you've got to hear it played
  by a good Brass Band

Pop and jazz and rock,
  and swing from many parts.
I've seen 'em all performed
  by big names at top o't charts.
But you ask any one of 'em
  where they want a one night stand,
an all of 'em 'll tell you
  with a really good Brass Band

Scottish reels and Irish jigs,
  African tribal dances,
and the occasional manic extrovert
  doing anything he fancies,
and even whirling dervishes
  I'm sure you'll understand,
would all prefer accompaniment
  from a really good Brass Band

The Sally Army's reet you know,
  they mek their music count.
When praising God they use it
  in just the right amount.
An' am sure reet from t'beginning
  in General Booth's first plans,
he provided for an Army with
  really good Brass Bands

If you get about eight cornets,
  euphoniums and basses,
some baritones and horns
  and four trombones in their places,
they'll play you 'owt you want,
  as long as it's on t'stand
and you'll nivver beat the sound
  of a good Brass Band

And when the final ***cornet*** sounds
  to call me up above,
I'll listen to the heavenly choir
  singing hymns of praise and love.
But I'll keep mi ears a'flapping
  for real proof of t'promised land,
the great, incomparable, sound
  of the heavenly Brass Band

T'Second Baritone's Lament *Loosely adapted from the'Alto's Lament'*

It's tough being Second Baritone
and playing in the band.
The cornets get the twiddly bits
that really sound quite grand.
The trombones horns and basses
all play with greatest glee.
But I'm just playing two notes,
. . .or if I'm lucky, three

And when the band plays really well
to earn the audience praises,
the horns get all the juicy bits
and telling little phrases.
Of course the cornets get the tune
and always come off best,
while I just get the same three notes
. . . and thirty-two bars rest.

It doesn't matter what I play,
or even how I play it,
Conductor's just to look at me
and then he's got to say it!
'Too high, too low, too fast, too slow;
you held that note too long'
It doesn't matter what I do
it's certain to be wrong

Oh, shed a tear for Baritone two's
they're martyrs, and they know,
that in the ranks of bandsmen
they're considered very low.
They are so very humble
that a lot of folks forget them.
They'd love to play a solo
but their playing skills
won't let them

So when the final trumpet sounds,
and we're all wafted higher;
while trombones, cornets,
horns and basses
play for t'heavenly choir,
accompanying t'Alleluias
with all the other bands,
. . . t'baritones will be in t'corner
mending t'music stands!

Yorkshire Born n' Bred

I've allus bin a Yorkshireman,
  Yorkshire born n' bred,
but try to be quiet modest
  so it dun't go to my head

But when you know you're
t'best in t'world,
  it's hard to keep it quiet.
If you tell a tyke to shut his mouth
  it's bound to start a riot

So I'll get mi pint o' Tetleys,
  and as I start to sip it,
I'll be thinking very hard
  about where to race mi whippet

Then off to t'pigeon loft I'll go
  to shoo the cats away,
then a dustbin-lid sized Yorkshire pud
  to see off t'end of t'day

Now lots o' folk think Yorkshire's
  all whippets and cloth caps,
and fish and chips, and clogs, and tripe,
  and quite broad-spoken chaps

But we're t'country's biggest county
  (as well as being t'best).
More acres than words in t'Bible,
  a cut above the rest.

If its scenery that you're after,
  then there are no buts or ifs
we've dales, and wolds,
  and mountains,
- and harbours, sea and cliffs.

There's Ingleboro', Whernside,
  (not forgetting Penyghent)
and miles of rolling countryside
  from Hull reet up to Dent

Harewood House
and t'Humber Bridge,
and Emmerdale and that,
  and t'Last of t'Summer Wine country,
and Ilkla Moor baht t'at

And then there's famous people -
  of them we're very proud.
We like to sing their praises,
  and sing 'em long and loud!

The Brontes, J.B.Priestley,
David Hockney, Henry Moore -
Some at'worlds best authors
and artists that's for sure

Trueman, Goughie, Boycott,
three lads from t'summer game.
Billie Whitelaw, Judy Dench -
acting's brought them fame

Of course, there's lots of others,
Dicky Bird, a perfect gent,
and that lovely, perfect English Rose,
our own Duchess of Kent

There's lots of famous Yorkshire folk
that meks us feel reet proud -
but you'll find a dozen unknown
gems in any Yorkshire crowd

I've allus been a Yorkshireman,
an' a Yorkshireman I'll dee,
and when I get to t'pearly gates,
St Peter'll say to me

'By gum lad, here you are at last;
you've finally made it then -
and just in time for t'cricket match,
it starts at half past ten'

'It's Yorkshire versus rest o t'world,
we play it every year,
and t'losers pay for all the drinks
so guess who gets t'free beer!'

Then Yorkshire'll mek 800 runs,
and t'world just 27,
and I'll be saying to mysen
'I really am in Heaven!'

But now back to reality -
feet firmly on the floor,
what is it meks a Yorkshireman?
I'll tell you that for sure

Now, your name is not important,
nor whether black or white.
If tha's been born i' Yorkshire,
you're a Yorkshireman bi right

Whether it's Robertshaw, or Clegg,
Kuminski, Joga Singh,
or Ali Khan or Jean Macnab,
you're Yorkshire, that's the thing!

So stand up for the old White Rose
Wherever you may go
For Yorkshire's God's own country
and He really ought to know!

A Tram to school

I were nobbat a lad of
abart fourteen years
  when I first started using the trams.
I'd got to, for that was the transport
for school;
  cars were scarce and there weren't
  traffic jams

The traffic was light in them days y'see,
  and trams could rattle along -
so long as they stayed on the
tramtracks of course
  so t'tracks were made *very* strong

Now them as 'ave only travelled by car,
  or on t'bus as quiet as a lamb,
'ave no idea what an ordeal it was
  to go for a ride on a tram

From near where I lived, going down
towards school
  we'd got a blooming steep hill.
It's o'er fifty years since I travelled
that route,
  but by gum, I remember it still!

We'd crowd on an' climb up steps to
t'top deck,
  like hooligans rather than vicars
and we'd go up behind a lass
if we could,
  for a glimpse of her
  navy blue knickers!

By gum, we were naughty
in them days,
  we'd watch women
  hanging out smalls,
and flatten out pennies on t'tram lines,
  and even write 'bum' on the walls!

But let's get back to the tramcar,
  now trundling on down the hill,
Tekking dozens a' kid's down
to t' highschool
  Plus a few folks just going to t'mill

Now upstairs on 'trams
I'm talking about
there were two different options
to choose;
undercover in t'middle
or oppen each end
and t'seats were as hard
as church pews

But in t'oppen it didn't really matter,
for in t'space of about
twelve square feet
some twenty or more kids were
standing,
and they totally ignored every seat

The timid would normally be outside
at back
but toughies would stand at the front,
braving the wind and the rain
and the snow -
and bruises in case of a shunt!

As the tram rattled quickly on down
the track
there was always excitement assured;
chucking rubbish at walkers,
ringing the bell,
and altering t'route number board

Excitement would grow as we went
down the hill
and nearer to t'dreaded Cliffe Bank.
The swaying increased and the tram
bucked and rolled,
just like a Challenger tank

On a bad day you'd even feel t'tram
leave the tracks
- at least that's what we believed,
so when we braked and slowed
down for school,
we were secretly all quite relieved

With an absolute lack of decorum
we streamed down the tram steps
pell-mell,
an' as soon as we'd passed the
conductor
we'd stamp on the tram's
warning bell!

Then we'd all stream off leaving
chaos behind
And t'conductor and driver
would sigh,
then set off again up the hill
in the tram
shouting 'thanks very much
- and goodbye!'

A Train to Morecambe

Whenever I've got time to spare
 You'll find me on a plane,
or on a bus, or on a boat,
 but specially on a train

For though I'm always on the move,
 It's a sort of Holy Grail
to travel here, there, everywhere,
 if possible, by rail

It started many years ago
 t'was in the days of steam.
Whenever trains were mentioned
 mi little eyes would gleam

Usually it were to Morecambe,
 either t'week or just for t' day,
Until I'd been so many times
 I knew each inch ot way

We'd tak a tram down into town, -
 another little thrill, -
walk into Bratford station
 and hear the whistles shrill

The smell o' steam were everyweer
 and t'station really packed.
Now't more exciting in the world
 for a ten-year-old in fact

We'd climb aboard and slam the door,
 lift winder wi' a strap;
one mum, one dad, and with 'em
 one excited little chap

Woo Woooo,
the engine's whistle screeched,
 and smoothly we'd depart.
Another epic journey was
 just about to start!

Chuff Chuff, Chuff Chuff,
the engine went,
 and t'wheels tit tat, tit tat,
while mum and dad just sat theer,
 doing nowt but chewing t'fat

But as for me, mi eyes were glued
 on t'cows, and sheep, and grass,
for there weren't no country where
we lived -
 just streets and t'smell of gas

I luvved the Hall's Distemper signs,
  two men with plank between;
striding out across the fields
  so beautiful and green

I knew all t'stations off by heart
  'Bell Busk' I luvved to say,
and when we got to Hellifield
  I knew we'd reached halfway!

And all the time the smell of steam
  as t'pistons clanked and hissed.
Them folks who's under 50
  just don't know what they've missed!

There were lots to see,
like railwaymen
  who'd look at t'wheels and tap 'em.
And we always laughed
at Giggleswick
  and then clapped hands at Clapham

And as the coaches rocked about
  and t'wheels went tat-ti-tat
you really got the feel of speed
  -doing 45, if that!

Now most of t' coaches had a snag
  I think you will agree.
They didn't have a toilet
  so you couldn't have a wee!

And as the journey took two hours,
  and t'stops weren't long enough,
unless you'd been before you went
  you'd find it pretty tough!

Now when we got to Hornby
  I had this fixed idea,
that all the model trains in t'world
  were manufactured theer

The next stop was at Lancaster
  an' if River Lune were low,
you knew for sure that tide was out
  at Morecambe, don't you know?

Then there on t' great long
curving bridge,
  if you looked through t'winder hard,
you'd see each single coach on t'train
  from t'engine reet tut' guard

Well, at last we got to Morecambe
  and all piled out ot' door,
and rushed through t'station exit
  to see the sea and shore

But sea, and sand, and t'donkeys,
  were really all i' vain,
for all that I looked forward to
  was steaming back again!

Fred's Burger Joint

That day I felt quite peckish,
  I were deeing for a bite;
then 'Fred's Burger's' sign flashed out,
  quite a welcome sight

I couldn't see another caff
  or restaurant anywhere,
so made me mind up and went in
  and found mi'sen a chair

Now I usually eat at restaurants
  or at a decent pub,
a proper Egan Rony man
  when it comes to scoffing grub

I also like mi fish and chips
  (Harry Ramsdens, crisp 'n 'ot)
and either coffee, tea or wine
  I'm drinking like as not

I couldn't find the menu
  so I sat upon mi' chair
and looked around for t'waiter -
  but there weren't one anywhere

It appeared that at this sort o' place
  the way to get your nosh
was to queue and pay at t'counter,
  which isn't very posh

Now I thowt when seeing t'tables
  they were a trifle bare,
no crockery or tablecloths,
  nor even cutl'ry there

But when I got my order,
  I found it very drastic
to see that all mi' food and drink
  was packed in card and plastic

Not a sign o' silverware
  or a bit o' fine bone china.
No, card and paper were the thing
  in this partic'lar diner

The choice I'd found quite baffling -
  Singles, Trebles, Doubles;
plus 'Superburgers' (veg or cheese),
  an' this added to mi troubles

But scanning t'coloured pictures,
  I had a real long think,
an' ordered t' Superburger
  an' a cup of coke to drink

I'd ordered with me burger
  some things they called French
Fries.
A box of undernourished chips,
  I found to my surprise

Now as a new boy at this game
  I were used to quails in aspic,
an' rack o' lamb, an' syllabub
  not chips in flippin' plastic!

But as I struggled with the food
  and t'coke in t'cardboard cup,
I admitted that with all its faults
  it really filled me up!

Well some folks think
that sort of food
  can really be a treat,
but I'm a bit up market
  about the things I eat

Next week I'm on a gourmet's binge,
  I'll do six restaurant trips.
And then I'll maybe finish t'week
  wi' Ramsdens fish and chips

On your 60th birthday

When you get to sixty,
  the whole world's at your feet.
A host of new experiences
  are there for you to meet

Hernia, weak bladder'
  high blood pressure and cramp,
arthritis, coughs and breathlessness
  and you're sensitive to damp!

But don't despair, for as you know,
  only five years t' the pension
(cheap buses, trains and theatres
  are other perks I'll mention)

So hang on there, there's lots left yet
  it could be quite exciting,
a life brim full of energy,
  playing draughts and letter writing

You might aspire to carpet bowls
  if you can leave your chair,
an' if you can't, then nivver mind,
  you can knit just sitting there

So go ahead, enjoy your age;
  make sure you have some fun,
because before you know it,
  you'll find you're sixty-one!

T'Great Marra' Mystery

It t'were t'day of the Cobblebeck
annual show.
  Folks were turning up
  in their dozens.
Mothers, fathers, a sprinkling o' kids,
  and aunties, and uncles, and cousins

They were milling abart and
lookin' at vases
  with all sorts of flowers on show -
and veg very tastefully done up i'sets,
  in row after row after row

But the focus of all the attention
  was on a rather large barra',
and there on a g't big cushion of straw
were Joe's quite enormous great marra'

Joe Crump had won t'prize for 't'Best
of the Show',
  for as long as I can remember
the only important date in his year
  were that third week-end
  i' September

Now I'm not a marra' man
really, misen,
  don't fancy gardening that much -
in fact soil and mulch and garden
manure
  I find quite revolting to touch

But I've often wondered
about Joe's success.
  How he allus captures first prize.
How he nurtures and grows a tiny
young pip
  to such a gobsmackin' size

An' on all t'occasions I'd asked him,
  reply'd been obscure, sometimes silly;
all about his success being due
  to his offspring, 'our little Willie'

Now 'our little Willie', Joe's little lad
  will be nine or possibly ten,
so I asked Joe once more if he'd
like to expound
  but I got t'same reply once again

At this point 'Miss Marples' just
came to mind,
  and other great sleuths down
  through history.
I decided I'd be a detective
  and solve the 'Great Marra' Mystery'

Well, I read all the books on gardens
I could -
  messed wi' leaf mould and even
  cow muck.
Studied temperatures, wattering
and 'hotbeds',
But didn't have very much luck

Now possibly t'best of all t'methods
I'd studied
  (an' the work I can say
  drove me frantic)
might give you a fairly big marra',
  but not one that's really gigantic

No, there really had to be summat else
  besides the heat and manure,
but Joe still gave t'credit to
'our little Willie'
  and he'd nivver tell me no more

I prowled near t'allotment
for hour after hour
  wi' binoculars, cameras, the lot -
I could just as well a'been
sitting at home,
  for all t'satisfaction I got

And still Joe protested
he didn't do owt
  that were out of the ordinary like,
but said he relied on 'our little Willie'
  and 'on his rusty old bike'

'Aha' I thowt 'there's a clue here
no doubt',
  as I listened to Joe's last remark,
but though I tried to fathom it out,
  at t'show I were still in the dark

And then looking round whilst
speeches were on,
  I saw Joe round t'back of his marra'
bent almost double in pain,
that he was,
  just as though he'd been struck
  by an arra'

It were one o' them arthritic twinges
  that Joe seemed nivver to suffer -
except at t'horticultural show,
  where it made him look a reet duffer

And then, by gum, in a blinding flash,
  I realised I suddenly knew
how Joe produced his g't marra' -
  at last I'd tippled to t'clue

I plunged me 'and into
t'cushion o'straw,
  and I've nivver felt such a chump,
but there plugged in
t' back o' the marra'
  were Willie's old bicycle pump

So there were the secret
in t'oppen at last
  Joe's bending wasn't rheumatic.
He was just givin t'marra'
it's next bit o' wind
  Joe's success was purely pneumatic

Well, now it were curtains
for Crumpy,
  he left the tent in disgrace,
and nivver again at Cobblebeck Show
  did he ever so much show his face

And as for 'our little Willie',
n' more dare he ride t'bike at all,
and the nickname he earned, 'windy
marra'
drove him reet up the wall

Our Church photocopier

Our church photocopier's
a mind of its own,
  It moves in mysterious ways.
Sometimes it works like clockwork -
  that's on one of its better days

You'd think that a copier would just
stop or go
  and that'd be t'end o' the matter,
but ours is the devil incarnate,
  hence the reason I'm having this natter

For instance it teks so long to warm up
  you could go home
  and have a good nosh,
read the paper and
watch the 6 o'clock news,
  and even have time for a wash

Then ***when*** it performs it does
marvellous tricks,
like acting just like a shredder,
and as you try to cope with its whims,
yer face gets redder and redder

I'm sick of forever oppening 'top
when all t'little leets start a'glowing.
It's like Blackpool Illuminations
gone mad
before I get the thing going

Then when you finally think it's OK
and it's churning out copies all right,
how ever you try to set 'controls,
they're either t'dark or t'light

Of course it's getting quite
long in the tooth,
ten or twelve years old it'll be
But thats no excuse, we're all getting on,
missen, I'm near seventy three

Now while I've been sitting here
writing this poem
the copier's been churning out sheets.
All wi' little black lines
down t' middle.
Just one more of its marvellous feats

But with a fiddle, an' a bit of a kick,
it's apparently OK again
the copies have all started flowing -
an I've managed to do nine or ten!

So at last things seem to be moving,
and I've only three hundred to
print;
with luck I'll be home in an hour
after doing this marathon stint

But no, once again
the machine's gone berserk;
the ink container's run dry;
an' umpteen copies
are stuck in the rollers,
by gum, I just want to cry

In the hundreds of hours I've used
this machine
I've cussed it,
used many a rude name,
an' now most likely
I'll not get to heaven
an' there's only missen I can blame

And the problem of having
fallen from grace,
when I dee,
and they're tolling the bell,
is I'll finally come once more face to face
wi' that photocopier from Hell

Be Prepared

The first time I went camping
  were during World War II.
I'd been in t'scouts a year or more,
  but camping was quite new

We didn't camp in just one place
  nor did we go by bus
but dragged a heavy Trek Cart round
  just five or six of us

Our first stop was on t'Chevin Top.
  just seven miles from home.
When we arrived we ached so much
  we felt we'd walked fro' Rome!

We pitched our tents and made a fire,
  and started on wi't food -
spuds boiled along wi'sausages;
  by gum, it wer'n't half good!

As soon as dusk began to fall
  after such a busy day,
by heck, we were so tired
  that we dropped off straight away

The next day - up at 6am
  (we'd planned an early start,)
and started loading up our gear
  onto the old trek cart

We dragged the cart t' top of t'hill
  that dropped down into town,
then straining back with all our might,
  we gradually eased it down

We're doing rather well', we thowt
  'at managing this load',
when suddenly a wheel fell off
  and rolled away down t'road

Well, two of us ran after it,
  some hundred yards down t'lane,
and finally we caught up wi' it
  and hauled it back again

A half an hour to mek t'repair,
  and off we went once more,
a mere eight miles to Asquith
  though it seemed a darn sight more!

We got our camp set up though,
  and made a cup of tea,
before a stroll around the woods
  to see what we could see

A little way above our camp,
  we found t'dead sheep in t'stream-
the stream we'd used to brew our tea!
This quite upset the team!

But suffering no ill effects,
  we stayed another day,
then packed our stuff upon the cart
  and set off on our way

Dick Hudson's was a nine mile trek
  on t'road reet ovver t'moor,
and I can tell you by this time
  our feet were very sore!

Now when it came to tea time,
suet pudding was the talk,
and we had a cook who volunteered
whilst t'rest went for a walk

But although away at least an hour,
the pudding hadn't thickened,
and told we'd have to wait for tea,
we all felt fairly sickened

Another hour, and still not done,
we said we had to eat,
and demolished t'suet pudding,
and voted it a treat !

But came the dawn, I roused myself,
to check out Trek Cart hub
and peeped into the little tent
which housed our stores and grub

Imagine my surprise, then,
to find the 'flour' for t' pudd
wasn't really flour at all,
- it wasn't even food!

No, the 'flour' was nobbut plaster,
that we'd browt to get a cast
of animals little footprints,
not to relieve our fast

Well, when everyone
had been informed
about this dreadful thing,
we all began to wonder
as to what the day would bring

Would the plaster set inside?
Would it bung us up?
might it make a difference
if we had a lot to sup?

So we drank at least a gallon each
in the hope we'd flush it out,
then set off on t' final leg,
each one a worried Scout

Well, with all that watter in us
(just 'tween you and me)
we must have stopped a hundred
times
while someone had a wee!

But finally we got back home,
and no one seemed affected,
by the dreaded seize-up
that everyone expected!

The Trek Cart back in t'Scout Hut,
it was then the family beckoned.
There were lots o' stories
we could tell
a few more than we'd reckoned!

I did all this at twelve years old,
a great adventure shared,
and whatever came in t'future,
I knew I'd Be Prepared!

T' Ow'd Bradford Coit of Arms

Newfangled Bradford got new Coit
of Arms
  in Nineteen Seventy Four,
when at last it became Metropolitan,
and not just a City no more

But long before that in medeevil times
  Bradford were really quite small,
and there weren't any football or rugby,
  in fact no games played at all

There was a bit of hunting of course
  not foxes, but wolves, boars
  and bears,
and you killed 'em wi' arrers or
spears or big swords,
  after tracking 'em down to their lairs

Now if tha's leaving our town
for the north,
  (an' I hope you're not going for good)
tha'll see a big hill by t'main road
ont' reet,
  formerly known as Cliffe Wood

It was in this big wood there lived a
huge beast,
  a beast so fierce and so big,
that everyone laughed when 'them in
the know'
  said 'Nay, its nobbut a pig'

Pedantically speaking, a porker it was,
but not the domestic variety.
No, this was quite wild, a g't boar
no less,
and quite a threat to society

It rampaged about killing
'owt it could find,
then poked and prodded in t'mud.
It scared t'local peasantry near
half to death -
and it didn't do t'gentry much good!

So Edwin de Lacy,
the boss hereabouts,
said whoever could kill this owd boar,
would receive a very large prize
for his work,
but surprising, response were
quite poor

Except for John Northrop, a brave
lad from town
who set out to do the great deed;
after all, it wan't just glory he sought
he'd a wife and six kids to feed

He tracked t'boar down to its lair
near a well,
in the densest part of the wood.
He unsheathed his sword and leapt
at the beast,
and did for t'owd tusker for good

Now, having done t'deed he found
that the boar
was much too heavy by far,
and as he lived in medeevil times
he hadn't the use of a car

So thinking like lightning he took art
his knife,
cut off the tongue in t'boar's gob,
then popped to his home for a quick
cup o' tea
an' a warm for his feet up on t'hob

Now during the time he were having
his tea,
along through the wood came
young Fred.
A lad with always an eye for
t'main chance
he saw t'boar and whipped
off its head

He were what you'd call now
an en-tre-pre-neur,
ready to make a fast buck.
So he dragged t'head off to t'Lord o'
the Manor,
hardly believing his luck

But when Edwin looked reet in
t'boar's mouth
 and found its tongue were
 quite gone,
he asked our Fred to account for
himself
 and answer from Fred
 came there none

Tea finished, our hero John Northrop
set off
 to claim the real star prize,
confronting young Fred and waving
the tongue,
 thus bringing the lad down to size

So Ed banished Fred, and then
turned to John
 and said 'I've run out o' jam,
but I've got you a nice little
parcel of land -
 I'm giving you all Manningham'*

'And that's not all,' said our Edwin,
 'I've also run out of crumpet,
but get a grip on this lovely ram's 'orn,
 it'll mek thee a very good trumpet'

** Another version of the story mentions Great Horton*

'I'll give you the trumpet
quite willingly
 on a very important condition.
You blow it three times on
Martinmas day
 who knows, it could start a tradition'

And so to this day the story is told,
 and in essence you'll find
 it's quite true,
though you might get
a difference i' detail
 depending on who you talk to

An if tha looks at t'owd Coit of Arms,
 you'll see there, at 'top, big and bold,
boars 'eead, mouth oppen,
and minus a tongue,
 just like the story I've told

And then lower down if tha' looks
tha should see
 a shield wi' three 'orns and a well,
a sure confirmation of t'story
 I've just had the pleasure to tell

Although t'Coit of Arms is now quite
defunct,
 its a story that's well worth recall,
so I thowt I 'd write and record it,
 for them that don't know it at all

T'Messiah *Adapted from a traditional prose monologue. As in the original monologue, the musical sequences depart somewhat from the score.*

One day I were passing
St Georges Hall
  when a bright poster
  just caught my eye.
T' were all about t' thing called
t' Messiah,
  so I thought I'd give it a try

So come last December on
one Friday neet,
  I joined a long bustling queue,
and found t' hall were crowded and
choc full o' folk,
  though for what, I still hadn't a clue !

Now as soon as I saw as how they
were dressed,
  for t' most part in boiled shirts
  and bow ties,
I decided to tak off mi muffler and cap
  and make sure I'd done up mi flies.

For t' women were even more dressed
up than t' men,
  In dresses I'd say were quite naughty.
When I found myself staring at one
woman's chest,
  her reaction were really quite haughty !

Well, then a chap started
la'akin on t' organ
  in a very peculiar manner.
He sounded just like our Penelope did
  when she'd just started
  learning t'piana.

But then there were sort of a climax,
  as they brought on t' Messiah,
  (so I guessed).
It were t' biggest instrument
on t' platform that neet
  - a gert fiddle far too big for thi chest.

A fella got od, and producing a bow,
  he rubbed it across t' monster's belly.
By gum, you'd nivver believe
how it groaned -
  you'll nivver hear owt like it on telly !

He didn't seem really
pleased wi' it though,
  and he started experimenting like,
by twitching its earoil,
until I could swear
  that they'd actually hear it i' Wyke !

Well, then there appeared a chap
wi' a stick,
  and t' audience started to clap,
but soon he made signs
to tell 'em to stop,
  and unfolded what looked like a map

Then plonking this down on his
own little desk,
  he went at it like hammer and tongs,
and t' band and all t' singers
suddenly struck up
  and let everything rip
  wi' some songs.

Now its my firm opinion
  he should 'ave been stricter
wi' most of that lot in the choir,
  for before very long they were
  fratching like cats,
wi' their voices going
higher and higher.

First one side said
  'We're t' King of Glory',
then t' other side said
'nay, you're not'
  They didn't seem able to settle it
 -as for me I'd have sacked the
whole lot !

Well they went from one thing
to another,
  and't' sheep' were t' next thing
  they'd to do.
It seems they were lost,
and judging by t' noise,
  choir were probably lost too.

Now this lot of singers were
real fond o' mutton,
  'cos now they sang 'All we like sheep'
They just sang it ovver and ovver again,
  'till I thought they'd collapse in a heap.

I couldn't help saying
to t' chap next to me
  'Y'knaw, sheep's all reet for
  a change,
but you can't beat a bit of
well-done scrag-end
  cooked on an old oppen range'

Well, do you knaw,
he looked daggers at me,
  and whispered
  'Please will you be quiet'
You'd have thought from the way he
told me to shush
  I was keen on starting a riot !

Anyroad, just then a big chap gorup,
  took a big breath, and started to sing.
By, I wish you'd been theer
to hear him !
  He made everything go with a zing !

He sounded as mad as old blazes
  as he sang about t' Heathen all raging,
wi ' t' fiddles all sagging and sawing,
and conductor all swishing and waving

But being a long time since it started,
  by now I were getting quite stalled,
when a bloke wi' a really long trumpet
  played a bit that had me enthralled

'Trumpet shall sound' 's what they
called it,
  eckythump, it fair woke me up -
and then all t' audience started to stand,
  an' I thought to missen
  'now what's up ?'

Now the thing that had made 'em all
ger on their feet
  were to see all the singers do t' same,
as they sang a thumping big chorus
  'Hallelujah', that were its name

By gum, it were reet grand to hear it,
  an' for me it were quite a new trend.
Mi back went into cold shivers,
  and then all mi hair stood on end !

It came as a really big climax,
  as mi back continued to quiver,
and t' choir all sung that
now it were barn
  to 'rain for ivver and ivver' !

Well, at t'end I'd had me full
bobsworth.
  It really had been quite a neet.
I were thinking I'd really enjoyed it
  as I pushed mi way out on t' street.

But in view of what choir had said
about rain,
  though I'm really quite a tough fellah,
I made mi way ovver to t' bus double
quick,
  as I'd clean forgot mi umbrella !

Land of Hope and Glory

I've just had a weekend i' London,
it were quite an adventure for me.
I usually spend weekends much
closer to home -
too fond of mi comforts you see

But t'reason for t'visit were special
It were summat I'd heard all about -
the last neet at Proms,
no more and no less,
tha knaws, weer they sing
and they shout

Now old Albert Hall were a good
mate o' mine
so I were quite surprised to find out
it weren't him, but a place
for the concert
that folks had been talking about

Well I got in, sat down and
waited a bit
then up bi t'organ i' rows,
appeared a g't group
of women and men
dressed up in all their best clothes

Then following t'choir, (for that's who
they were)
came folks carrying fiddles
and basses,
and dressed like a lotta big penguins,
with superior smiles on their faces

An' as well as carrying
fiddles and stuff,
they had trombones and flutes
and suchlike
But I reckoned however good that
they were,
they wu'nt be a patch on t'Black Dyke

Well, t'conductor appeared and got art
his stick,
and took a good look at the tune,
then ordered his choir into action,
just like an army platoon

Some notes were high, some notes
were low,
but t'choir seemed to manage all reet,
and by 'time they'd stopped
their carousing,
I were ready for t'rest of the neet

Then t'band played a few little bits on
their own,
and first half went wi' a swing,
and when it came to the interval
I were quite enjoying t'whole thing

But after we'd all got back in our seats
the music got more patriotic,
and t'behaviour of 'teenagers up near
the front
got more and more chaotic

Then on comes a woman in red white
and blue,
at least six foot two standing up
by gum, she'd arms like a navvy,
an' her bust were at least a 'D' cup

Now when she appeared
t'excitement were tense,
 as we knew the climax were near,
and t'audience lost all their decorum,
 and started to clap and to cheer

Standing so proud and so statuesque,
 with a voice that had t'crowd
 quite aghast,
she started the first of her pieces -
 'Rule Britannia' sung at full blast

Banners were waved and t'balloons
went off 'pop'
 but by gum, she just kept on going
Missen I'd 'ave stopped and had a
harsh word
 at all this to-ing and fro-ing

But no, she went on t' t'end o' the piece,
 and received tumultuous applause -
and a kiss on the hand
from t'conductor -
 after which we had a slight pause

And then what we'd waited for since
we'd arrived
 'Land-of-Hope-and-Glory'
en-cap-sul-ating, as it were
 Britain's marvellous story

Well, bi' t'end I were theer wi tears in
mi eyes,
 and couldn't stop blowing mi nose
I felt mi hair start to stand up on end,
 an' mi legs tingled down to mi toes

And now looking back on a
cracking two days,
 I'd had a blooming good time.
I'd started by booking my tickets
on t'net;
 by, that Microsoft system is fine

I'd a safe drive to London in t'Fiat
 (Mich'lin tyres are as good as they say)
Stopping just once to fill up with Esso,
 (and Kentucky Fried Chicken)
 on' t'way

Then in London I'd meals at
Macdonalds,
 washed down bi gallons of Coke
I were tempted to puff
at a Marlborough -
 but as you know, I don't smoke

I stopped in a pub for a couple o' jars,
 a Carlesberg and a Budweiser
then in t'cinema watching
a Hollywood film
 I'd a Pepsi (they didn't stock Tizer)

The Toshiba TV in t'Hilton hotel
 were perfect to watch late at night,
an' as for mi snapshots on t'Pentax,
 they're Kodak so they'll be all right

By gum what a cracking old weekend,
 and I hope you don't think
 that I'm skittish,
but Kodak, Fiat, Toshiba and stuff!
 Should I really be proud
 to be British?

The meaning of Christmas

Our Christmas began on July 21st,
at a Car Boot Sale on one Sunday.
For that's when we bought
a great pile o' cards,
and we wrote 'em
the following Monday.
Some of the cards were quite funny,
and some of 'em really quite rude;
on one a reindeer stuck on a roof,
on another a girl in the nude

There wasn't the real Christmas spirit,
much too early I think you'll agree,
but even then something was missing,
and I wondered what it could be

We were buying like mad by October,
for Christmas, the real big event.
We were spending money like watter,
as though it were all heaven sent.
We were still rushing round
in November,
I mean that's what it's really about.
If we bought our friends lots of presents
we'd get a lot back I'd no doubt

By now I'd have thought we'd have
just about felt
a bit of excitement and glee.
But still something seemed
to be missing,
and I wondered what it could be

By December the 5th, still at it,
getting lager and whisky and wine,
and vodka and cider and brandy;
by, we'd all have a really good time.
On December 16th we'd the turkey,
and stuffing and plum duff - a must;
for what is the meaning of Christmas
if you can't stuff yourself fit to bust?

Yet still I felt quite unexcited;
it had gone on for year after year.
Something always seemed
to be missing.
I thought it was all rather queer.

Came the day and we threw a big party.
  Stuffed in food, and smoked
  lots of cigs,
played games and
drank ourselves silly,
  in fact generally behaved
  just like pigs.
Well, I 'd done me best, and I'd
spent lots o' cash
  to make Christmas go with a swing.
I'd crackers and mistletoe,
holly and wine,
  I don't think I missed anything.

We'd even got lots of bright tinsel
  and a fairy on 'top of the tree,
and yet the whole thing left me flat
and depressed,
  and I wondered just why
  that could be

Then, after our guests had departed,
  out a t'window when just passing by
I saw a truly magnificent star,
  lighting the frosty night sky.
Then somewhere inside me
a memory stirred,
  and back and back the years rolled
to a simple Christmas long long ago
  and a story my mother had told.

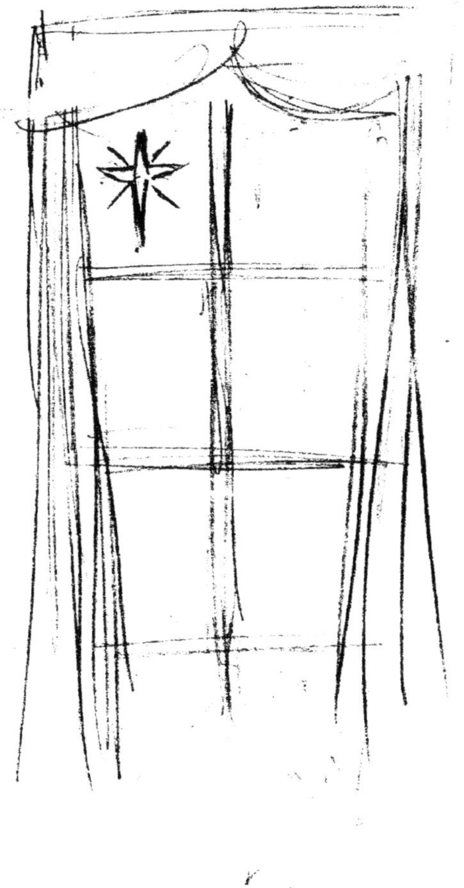

A story of angels and shepherds
  then the light began to dawn!
yes, that's the ***real***
meaning of Christmas
  it was then that Jesus was born!

Nativity *(some liberties have been taken with the Biblical sequence of events)*

It were cold and quite bleak there i' winter
and t'shepherds just didn't want to know,
'cos t'sheep were all scattered on t'hillside,
and t'hillside all scattered wi' snow

Now one little fella' called Nathan
were just looking up at the sky,
when down floats a
nightie clad angel;
'Hello' he said - 'Just passing by'

'But before I go I've to tell thee,
of a really stupendous affair.
The Messiah is being born anytime,
i' Bethlehem - mek sure that you're there!"

And then with a wave he departed,
Zooming reet up into t'sky,
Whilst t'shepherds heerd
'eavenly voices
singing 'Glory to God upon High'

'What's Messiah?' said Nathan to t'others,
but no one had even a clue,
'cos there weren't Christmas Carols in them days,
and t'story was really quite new

But they thowt that it must be important,
as t'angels had told 'em to go,
so they voted and got a majority -
five yes's and only one no

They'd only just started on t'journey,
when what did they see on the road,
but three posh blokes wi'
their servants,
- each servant carrying a big load

These posh chaps they really were something
- two on camels and one on an 'orse.
They said 'We're three Kings from the Orient'
and t'shepherds all answered
'of course'

So they travelled along t'road together,
companions from near and from far;
it were easy to know the direction,
for they followed a
blooming great star!

At long last they reached
little Bethlehem,
and got to what seemed
the reet place,
- outside a large inn full of trippers,
all eating and feeding their face.

'Can you tell me if there's
a small baby?'
  said one of the Kings to a guest.
'Aye lad, in t'barn round the back like,
  wi't donkeys and t'chickens and t'rest'

They followed to weer
he were pointing
  and saw quite a humbling sight;
a dad, and a mum, and a baby,
  lodged in the stable for t'night

Now Nathan had feet that
were hurting,
  for that night they'd come quite
  a long way,
and as he'd said nowt on the journey,
  he felt now he'd summat to say

'Well, t'nursery's nowt to write
home about
  - just a shed at the side of a pub,
with asses and donkeys and bullocks
  - and t'whole place could do with
  a scrub!'

'But t'mother, she looks really lovely,
  though she must be quite tired,
  that I know
and although I can't really believe it,
  round t'baby there's sort of a glow'

'That's 'cos he's t'Messiah'
said Melchior.
  (He were one of the Kings
  we are told)
'We've all come with presents
for t'baby
  - here's mine, a big crown of gold,'

Then t'other two Kings gave
their presents
  before they proceeded to leave,
whilst Nathan, quite touched
by t'occasion,
  wiped the tears from his eyes
  on his sleeve

Now t'shepherds had all got
a problem,
  as they'd never given a thought
as to how they should greet
this small baby,
  and presents were t'last thing
  they'd brought

However, they looked
in their pockets,
  knowing anythings better than nowt,
- and in fact they all found
they had summat
  - 'cept Nathan, who couldn't
  find owt

Well the poor little chap were
heartbroken,
and felt insignificant and small.
All these folks had given
their presents,
and he'd given nothing at all

'He's a beautiful baby' said Nathan,
'and I'll tell you this for a start -
although I haven't a present,
I could love him with all of my heart'

'Go back to your hillside,' said Mary,
'in peace, and in love and in Joy,
for I'll always remember
with gladness
the love that you gave to my boy'

'And in years to come,' said Mary,
'You'll be proud to have played
your full part
as the first of the untold millions
who've given Christ Jesus
their heart,'

So when *you* all celebrate Christmas,
with parties and food on the table,
- just remember how
everything started,
- with love in a small humble stable